Simple Money

Finance Tools for the Post-Boomer Generations

JASON WEBB

Copyright © 2014 Jason Webb

All rights reserved.

ISBN: 1494878917
ISBN-13: 978-1494878917

DEDICATION

This is dedicated to my parents who instilled values for personal and financial responsibility. Without their support and guidance, I would not have had the opportunity to write, to travel, or pursue my dreams.

CONTENTS

	Acknowledgments	i
1	Introduction	1
2	Budgeting Basics	5
3	Cash Flow	12
4	Net Worth	17
5	Frequency	20
6	Case Studies	22
7	New Tenants	31

ACKNOWLEDGMENTS

Thanks to Jason B. for always being supportive in all my endeavors and ready for any adventure.

CHAPTER 1

INTRODUCTION

High School taught us to balance a checkbook but never taught us how to manage a credit card, or how to navigate purchasing a car or house we can afford, or how to realistically understand when we can splurge. This concise book will teach the simple tools needed.

Why should you care? You likely live in a metropolitan area and are better educated relative to the average American. You see a steady stream of high-end luxury cars driven by peers or friends, or perhaps even by yourself. Your coupled friends are buying dream homes filled with high-end amenities.

The "Keeping up with the Jones" complex is weighing on you, or worse, you do not even see how it impacts your decisions any more. Or, you are one of the millions of Americans struggling to make ends-meet and yet you see the flaunting of material stuffs all over town and are left wondering what you are doing wrong. Let me help you understand why you not only do not need these trappings but cannot actually afford them, in most circumstances – and same is true for many living the material life.

Along the way, I will dispel the usual guidelines that help justify spending habits. For example: spend no more than 28% of your income on housing payments; spend no more than 36% on all debt payments: cars, homes, credit cards, student loans; spend two month's salary on the engagement ring. These "rules" do not stand on their own, which is conveniently left out when your friends and family cite them.

Another data point for why you should care: let us take a look at the typical expenditures today as Millennials versus those of our parents in the 1980's. You will see a significant change in where our dollars are being spent – now a greater percentage on amenity-infused homes, luxury cars, and technology-laced expenses, of which portions are not actually 'required'. For example, from 1986 to 2010, housing expenditures grew 11 to 15% for home owners and renters respectively, adjusted for inflation[1].

Why am I qualified and why should you learn from me? I grew up in small-town Kansas and have spent a decade living in Kansas City. By no means is this city a large metropolis, but I have been fortunate to distill observations here coupled with years of work in New York, DC, and other large metros. I see too many people in their 20s to 40s trapped in their brand-based lifestyle, perpetually without an emergency fund, without progress on retirement savings, getting left behind, and blindly trusting an underfunded Social Security program will be their retirement safety net.

To start, let us step back and forget every shred of personal finance knowledge you have ever learned.

---

[1] http://www.bls.gov/opub/btn/volume-1/pdf/a-comparison-of-25-years-of-consumer-expenditures-by-homeowners-and-renters.pdf

Forget the anecdotes your friends and family reference. In the upcoming chapters I will give you simple straightforward models and three financial tools that enable you to know what you can realistically afford and understand how to live within your income. We will start with budgeting basics, then cash flow, then net worth. I will cover when each of these activities is needed and end with several case studies and the new tenants of financial responsibility for our modern world.

The model each of these personal finance tools is based on is best thought of as a series of "dials", or what I call the Dial Model. The biggest should be your household's gross income. This is typically the hardest to adjust as it requires finding a different job, an additional job, or starting your own endeavor.

An ideal model then has a "required expense" dial that includes all the contractually obligated money outflows you are responsible for each month: insurance costs, rent/mortgages, utilities, etc. These too are typically hard to adjust quickly but can be changed as contracts come to an end, like changing cell-phone carriers, moving to a more modest apartment, etc.

Discretionary spending should be a relatively small "dial" and the easiest to quickly adjust. Similar to how required expenses impact our ability to save in the long run, discretionary spending has a direct impact in the near-term to our savings – savings being the final "dial".

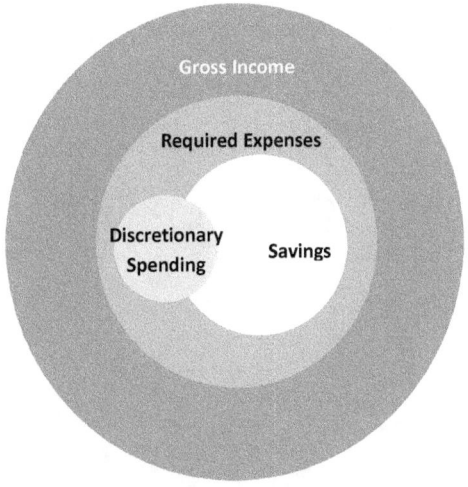

Dial Model – tracks the important relationships between income, obligated expenses, savings, and discretionary spending. Above is an ideal representation. Below is the more typical reality many have created to sustain lifestyle choices. The fundamentals and case studies will illustrate why dialing-in the below approach is inherently risky and not sustainable.

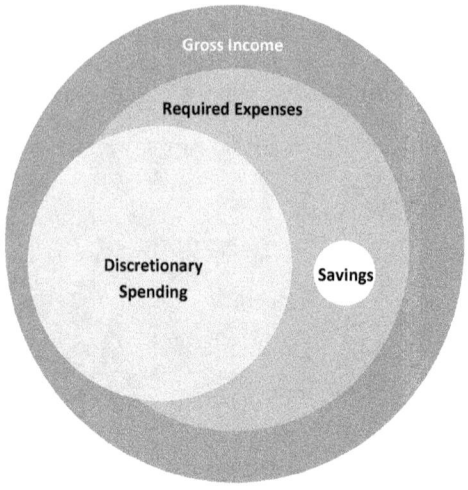

CHAPTER 2

BUDGETING BASICS

Grab a glass of wine, your favorite beer, or best spirit and let us work through the basics of budgeting, as painlessly as possible. The first step is to gather a copy of your most recent pay stub. If you are creating a family or household budget, then get the most recent pay stubs for all involved. For the freelancers and 1099 contract workers, the approach is similar and I will cover a couple of important caveats at the relevant points. Our goal is to first reinforce the concept of explicitly paying yourself before discretionary spending and second to identify what you realistically have available to splurge with after meeting all of your obligations.

Before we delve into math, let us spend a minute on that last word, obligations. Obligations are not eating out at fast food or dine-in restaurants, or getting drinks with your friends, or that weekend trip to see a distant old college roommate. People often have a perception that these lifestyle decisions in fact are not choices but are entitlements or are required. This mindset is one of the first mental models that you should forget. Obligations are expenses you are contractually obligated to pay. Your rent, your mortgage, a cell phone bill, a credit card are all examples of instances where you have signed a contract putting your credit score on the line based on an expectation you pay on time and in full for services or goods provided. Grabbing dinner and drinks with friends is a social contract. While important to keep your word, these are splurge expenses – and we need to understand what can reasonably be afforded while planning for important long term goals.

Grab that drink and take a big sip. Now for a bit of math to arrive at a monthly budget:

$ _____ Gross Pay: this is your total income before any deductions or taxes. If you get paid twice per month, multiply your pay stub numbers by two for this, the taxes, and deductions lines below. If you get paid every week or every other week, then step through the conversion to make a monthly gross pay number.

$ _____ Less Taxes: for many of you, federal, state and local taxes are automatically deducted from your paycheck.

Freelancer/1099er alert: you have the extra burden of estimating and setting aside funds for your tax obligations. You need to look at your approximate federal tax bracket (e.g. 15, 25, 28%), your Medicare / Social Security obligation, and your state tax bracket (e.g., 4, 5, 6%, etc.) and any applicable municipal earnings taxes. The total percentage you estimate is what you need to multiply your gross pay by to arrive at what amount of taxes to set aside.

$ _____ Less Payroll Deductions: if you have medical insurance, legal plans, and other automatic payroll deductions setup at your employer, subtract out the sum total of those obligations.

Freelancer/1099er alert: you likely have no automatic payroll deductions.

$ _____   Equals your Net Pay: this is what actually lands in your bank account.

$ _____   Less your Monthly Obligations: these are the payments you have contracted to make, such as credit cards, utilities, rent/mortgage, or you must make in order to survive, such as groceries. On this last point, groceries do not include eating out. Another important note here is past debt should be included in this category, such as student or car loans. I strongly advise you to avoid these burdens and will cover examples later in this

Freelancer/1099er alert: here you will likely include your medical insurance premiums and other expenses that others with corporate employers would have accounted for in automated payroll deductions.

book to further explain. Finally, credit cards are obligations in that you agreed to pay the issuing bank. However, aligning what you swipe to your actual budget is entirely up to you.

$ _____ Less Paying yourself: this should cover all of your savings needs and long-term goals, such as retirement, vacations, saving for a down payment on a house, a new car, an emergency fund, and required annual expenses (e.g. home or renters insurance, property tax payments, etc.). If you do not have an emergency fund that could cover all of the above expenses for not only 6 months but 18 to 24 months then that should receive your top priority ahead of the overwhelming majority of your "splurge" spending. In the economy of the last 5 years, many are finding job transitions taking many months. The 6 month duration of your emergency fund is insufficient in today's economic context. Beyond that, saving just 5 or 10% cannot reasonably cover your retirement and other needs for future vehicle and home upkeep/purchases. Think carefully about your long term goals here and arrive at an aggressive number that will ensure your financial security. Additional guidance is below.

$ _____ Equals your Monthly Discretionary Fund: this remainder covers all the extraneous things that are not required to stay fed and sheltered, and are not required to meet your long term financial goals. The discretionary fund covers your dining out, going to movies, the wedding gift for your best friend, your coffee addiction, your snowboarding/boating hobby, and any other extravagance you want to sprinkle in your life.

Try the exercise above for yourself. Remember to forget all you've learned before from friends and family and to forget your old budget. I think you will be surprised about the results. You are likely to see conflict between your "splurge" expenses, your savings, and your obligations. Many who lease a car will find they are sacrificing their long term financial goals to live in-the-moment and have a status symbol. Similarly, that 28% mortgage payment is strangling your family's ability to adequately build a safety net and fund other critical financial goals. Just because the bank and car dealership are telling you "yes, you qualify", you must understand they say yes to make money not because it is actually in your best interest. The bottom line is you need to carefully think through long term goals to find the right balance of what to set aside for yourself for the future, how to wrangle in your obligations, and how to still have enough left over to enjoy today.

How do you determine how much to save? I recommend thinking through your annual one-time expenses and also your long term goals. Your one-time expenses on an annual basis are typically your property taxes and insurance for your home and vehicles. If you own a home or vehicle, I also suggest tagging money each month for ongoing property and vehicle maintenance. This will help cover a new air conditioner, or unexpected brake replacement. Long term goals can include saving for a down payment on a home, buying your next car, planning for children, taking a vacation and retirement. Know that home down payments are 20% for traditional mortgage products. You can still find options in the marketplace with lower down payments. However, my guidance is if the 20% down payment is unaffordable to you with a sufficient emergency fund left over, you should not be signing up for the responsibility of home ownership. Set a timeline when you want to have accumulated sufficient money for the full 20% down payment amount, work backwards into what savings amount that requires each month, and fit it into your budget.

The best financial advisors suggest never financing a depreciating asset like a vehicle. If you have to finance a car, you cannot afford it. Save and think carefully about your car purchases. I'll share a case study later in the book to further prove this point. I also suggest having incremental retirement savings outside of a company 401k. This gives you broader control over the investment vehicles and allows you to take advantage of Roth IRA contribution limits as well. The guidance I give here is exceptionally aggressive to some. After looking at these goals greater than 40% of your net pay can easily be consumed by savings if you are doing this right and have adequate control over obligations. That is a massive mind shift for many. Take a breath, take another sip of your drink and know you are one step closer to achieving your long term goals and living within your means.

After doing the monthly budgeting exercise, take a final step back and build an annualized version. Multiply your gross pay, taxes, deductions, net pay, liabilities, savings, and discretionary fund numbers by 12 months to understand exactly where your dollars go. Even more interesting is understanding the percentage breakdown of each category. You may find your liabilities are greater than 50% of your income, which is a clear sign it is time to re-evaluate required spending and how to reign in your obligations.

For more guidance, visit www.simplemoneythebook.com to download a free budget template.

CHAPTER 3

CASH FLOW – MANAGING CREDIT SUCCESSFULLY

The budget serves as a guide to ensure your big picture goals are being met by adequately setting aside money for important future expenses before any money is allocated to discretionary funds. This is one hurdle down and a step closer to comfortably living within your means.

The next challenge many face and are not taught how to manage well is how to introduce credit cards into the mix of monthly finances. Credit cards, whether bank-issued or from your favorite loyalty or in-store program, demand a high degree of personal responsibility and oversight.

Additionally, credit cards introduce a layer of complexity making it more difficult to look at your checking account balance and immediately understand whether you have remaining discretionary money. Let us take a look at how to get into a simple rhythm of truing up near term income with your budget and credit card obligations to successfully manage cash flow.

Once again, a bit of math:

$ _____ Current checking account balance. Note: this should be the balance for your household.

$ _____ Plus next net pay check amount, which is the same as line 4 from the budget calculation in the prior chapter

$ _____ Less monthly obligations from line 5 of the budget

calculations and less paying yourself from line 7 of the budget calculations. These cover long term savings goals and shelter and food obligations. I typically move savings dollars into a separate account that is difficult to immediately access. In our household, we maintain a separate joint account specifically to fund all of our joint housing, grocery, and utility obligations.

$ _____ Less credit card charges accumulated since the last statement date.

$ _____ Equals remaining account balance.

Sequence the above calculations to align with the dates that your paycheck is deposited and the dates your credit card charges are due so you have an accurate view of what funds are expected to be available in your account and you are guaranteed to be able to cover your card payments in full. Moreover, forecast out 2 to 4 pay periods so you do not just have two weeks of cash flow visibility but closer to two months. This will help you understand if you are overspending now which will hit you in 30 days when your credit card bill is due.

Here is an example to help illustrate the power of managing cash flow successfully, with credit cards in the mix of your personal finances. Assume that you are paid on the 1st and 15th of the month and you have a credit card bill due with a major bank on the 20th and another due on the 23rd.

Day

13th	Current checking account balance:	$3525.00
15th	Next net pay check amount:	$1575.00
15th	Less monthly obligations and savings:	$1200.00
20th	Less current credit charges (Bank 1):	$450.00

23rd Less current credit charges (Bank 2): $350.00
    Equals remaining account balance: $3100.00

In this example, notice the cash flow calculation is forcing you to assume full payment of the credit card charges so you can see when spending is outpacing income. Moreover, notice that in this example there is only $375 ($1575 in net pay less $1200 in obligations and savings) in discretionary spending per pay check yet $800 has been charged on credit cards. This is an immediate flag that credit card spending needs to be kept in check the rest of the month to not break the budget and to ensure an ability to pay the credit card bill in full and not take a 18 to 24 percent finance charge for the privilege of carrying a balance when you bought more than could be afforded.

Let us expand on the example above and now take a look at the same data points one week later and extend the view out an additional month:

Day

20th Current checking account balance: $3350.00

23rd Less current credit charges (Bank 2): $750.00

1st Next net pay check amount: $1575.00

1st	Less monthly obligations and savings:	$1200.00
15th	Next net pay check amount:	$1575.00
15th	Less monthly obligations and savings:	$1200.00
20th	Less current credit charges (Bank 1):	$800.00
23rd	Less current credit charges (Bank 2):	-
	Equals remaining account balance:	$2550.00

Notice that the Bank 1 credit card due on the 20th was paid in full ($450), that another $100 was removed from the ATM directly from the checking account, and that another $400 was charged to credit card at Bank 2 after an active week of dinners out and entertainment. Forecasting out to the next month, you'll see net pay and savings and obligations are included as well as an incremental $800 already charged on credit card with Bank 1. The trend emerging in the forecast checking account balance is clearly negative because of overspending on discretionary items. The only way to resolve is to re-balance lifestyle during the week to reduce spending. If this is not corrected, the credit card bills will not be able to paid in full and then debt will start to build that is exceptionally difficult, and costly, to rectify.

Occasionally you will encounter a one-time annual

expense, like a property tax or insurance bill. To cover these, dip into the savings you have set aside from your previously determined budget. Say your car tax bill was $300 and it is due in two weeks. Pull $300 from the savings fund into checking, pay the bill and know the budgeted savings plan has accounted for the expense successfully.

After you have done the budgeting exercise, try this cash flow calculation for yourself. You may identify you are overspending on credit cards and cannot pay in full based on your current income. If this is your case, I won't mince words: you must take an immediate and careful look at your priorities to cut out unnecessary spending. Stop eating out and start using your kitchen. If your reaction is "what will my friends think?" they should be supportive of your new-found responsibility or they are not good friends. If you are worried about when you will see them, invite them over for dinner and drinks instead of going out.

For more guidance, visit www.simplemoneythebook.com to download a free cash flow template.

CHAPTER 4

NET WORTH

You have earned several long draws on that drink by now, if not a refill. Learning rather tedious financial concepts on your free time is a chore. The last step is to work through a statement of net worth. Fortunately, this is also the easiest concept in comparison to budgeting and cash flow. Here is what you need to make the calculation: a stack of all of your most recent account statements or web access to see current account balances.

Assets: add up all of your bank and investment account balances, plus the current market value of any other significant assets, like real estate. An easy and free real estate valuation resource is Zillow.com, though note the value displayed is only an estimate, may not be fully accurate, and does not remove the 5 to 6 percent transaction fee paid to realtors to sell the property. Kelly Blue Book can provide a similar guide to car resale value.

Liabilities: add up all of your outstanding payments, including credit cards, any mortgage debt, student debt, and vehicle debt, etc.

To get to Net Worth, subtract liabilities from assets. With any luck, there is a positive number.

There are instances when having a negative net worth is not only possible, but generally accepted. Many times, after the purchase of your first home, especially if transacted when young, there aren't many other assets that offset the remaining house liability. You are placing a bet that future income exclusively will drive your ability to pay the mortgage debt successfully. Similarly, many fresh from college or continued education will show a negative net worth that resulted from student loan debt. Here too, they are betting that future earnings will sufficiently cover debt payments over and above meeting long-term savings goals. While both of these scenarios are societally accepted nowadays – each is a significant bet that very limited job interruptions occur that would jeopardize debt payments. Given the economy of the past 5 years this is a huge bet for a younger generation who grew up in their parents dream homes and has a sense of entitlement to maintain that same lifestyle.

For a younger person still debating college, it is of critical importance in today's job market to have a clear vision and understanding of how to convert the expensive college degree into a tangible set of skills that are employable. For those who have already made this investment and are struggling with the payoff, it is of utmost importance to manage discretionary costs to continue the debt pay down as it will delay the ability to achieve other long term goals. College can be very useful, but only when coupled with the right set of real-world internship and work-study experiences that make you job-market relevant. Parents and students must push past the slick college marketing materials and make a legitimate assessment of how to recoup their investment to limit the risk of leaving with an overpriced piece of paper and no career opportunity.

If you are in a situation where you have accumulated debts on a home, vehicle, or student loans and are trying to work your way through, there are many options. Fundamentally, the budgeting and cash flow basics are the key tools. They can be supplemented with a simple loan amortization tool, a tool available at BankRate.com, to understand the total interest paid over the life of each loan for the remaining term, interest rate, and principal. If resources are constrained, I suggest ensuring credit cards are paid in full first and lifestyle adjustments are made to stop growing credit card debt as these typically carry the highest interest rates. Remaining debts can be prioritized to some extent based on interest rates with preference given to higher rate items. By preference I am not intending to say neglect your home payment because it is the lowest interest rate loan in your debt portfolio. Rather, I am saying it can make sense to accelerate loan repayment on higher interest loans to reduce overall interest due – so budget and pay extra.

Over the long term, net worth should turn positive and continue to grow. The end goal is to achieve the lifestyle you want in retirement with enough cushion to cover late life care. For retirement advice, there are enumerable options and nuggets of wisdom marketed. The bottom-line is when you are to that point in your life, you need to utilize the budget and cash flow techniques to continue to manage your finances while accounting for the change in income mix.

CHAPTER 5

HOW FREQUENTLY TO EXECUTE EACH FINANCIAL CONCEPT

We have now covered, budgeting, cash flow, and net worth calculations. One more key detail remains, and that is how frequently should you be compiling each financial metric to successfully steer your financial success.

Let us step through the frequency of each of these metrics from the least frequent to the most. The budget needs only to be generated once a year, or at major life events like job changes, new relationships, children, etc. This is your guide post that aims to keep you on track to achieving major long term financial goals.

Next most frequent is your net worth statement. You would be well served to compile this metric a couple of times a year to maintain a view of investment impacts to your portfolio and to provide an opportunity to modify your course. Certainly if you intend to be a more active investor, then the net worth statement becomes more important – at least on the asset side to understand investment performance, potentially as frequently as weekly.

Finally, the cash flow calculations are needed most frequently. I recommend identifying this metric on a weekly basis to keep close tabs on spending across credit cards and how future income and current liabilities align to identify available discretionary funds.

CHAPTER 6

CASE STUDIES

By now, you must be ready for a snack and a day dream about a future vacation. As thrilling as all the theory and math can be, to really drive home the relevance several case studies follow.

Case Study 1:

Meet Tara and John. They have a combined income of $90,000 with two elementary school aged children, a house in the suburbs for which they paid $200,000, two leased cars, and a boat for the summers. Their children are the light of their lives, though they sometimes wonder how college will get funded and dream about the bright futures they hope their children will have.

How does their budget work?

- Gross Monthly Income: $7,500
- Automatic Deductions for health insurance and taxes: $2,300
- Net Pay: $5,200
- Debt Obligations for cars, boat, and housing: $2,500
- Other required expenses (e.g. groceries, utilities, property insurance, etc.): $1,200
- Long-term goals (e.g. vacation, home repairs, car repairs, and retirement): $1,000
- Discretionary funds remaining: $500

Do you see any issues? While they are having fun and living the suburban life to the fullest, they are only putting away $1,000 of their monthly income, or less than 15%, for long-term goals. They are bleeding 33% of their gross income on debt payments to keep the newest cars, boats, and suburban home all up-to-date. The sacrifice being made is not for today but for their own future with an underfunded retirement account and an inability to respond to unexpected job loss or big ticket home or car repairs. Some may be comfortable taking on this risk but doing so is at the expense of the entire family's well-being in the future.

To illustrate further, let us assume Tara and John have $5,000 in emergency cash savings. If Sara lost her job, their monthly gross income would reduce $3,000. Health insurance costs would rise if they utilize a COBRA option and their debt obligations remain constant. They have 1 to 2 months before not all debts can be successfully paid – meaning that a car or boat become at-risk of repossession, or the house is at-risk of foreclosure.

How could this family mitigate risk better? This is largely a question of lifestyle choices – referencing back to the Dial model. Selling the boat and one of two leased vehicles would reduce required expenses. Finding a creative way to juggle for a couple of months a single vehicle should build enough cash to pay out-right for a reasonable used car. Yes, the luxury boating hobby and the fully-equipped car will be gone. However, in the case of an unexpected job loss, Tara and John's spending habits would allow them to at least maintain their revised lifestyle without risk of losing their home or vehicles. Recalibrating their required expense dials in the coming months is critical to meeting long-term financial goals.

Case Study 2:

Meet Jim. He graduated from college four years ago and recently received his first big promotion last year. He's earning $75,000 and living the life, well above the median American's income level. He is driving a beautiful new leased Audi A4. Jim has a year-long rental obligation at a downtown loft with the beautiful vaulted ceilings and a spare bedroom.

How does his budget work?

- Gross Monthly Income: $6,250
- Automatic Deductions for health insurance and taxes: $2,000
- Net Pay: $4,250
- Obligations for car and apartment: $2,000

- Other required expenses (e.g. groceries, utilities, rental insurance, student loan debt etc.): $900
- Long-term goals (e.g. vacation, home repairs, car repairs, and retirement): $300
- Discretionary funds remaining: $900

What risks do you see? Jim has managed to set aside some money in his company-matched savings plan for retirement and a modest $2,500 for emergencies. However, he is living the high life spending nearly $1,000 a month on entertainment – concerts, drinks and dinners out with friends, weekend trips. All are great for living in the present yet yield several key risks. What if something happened to his apartment, like a fire or water damage? He would have to come up with a $1,000+ renters insurance deductible, plus relocation costs that could quickly deplete cash savings. Going a step farther, what if his work position was eliminated? He could only sustain his $2,900 in required living expenses for a month without the job. His lifestyle choices have him living in the present with inadequate long-term savings contributions to navigate a financial hurdle successfully.

What should Jim do differently? He should make three changes to recalibrate lifestyle with his actual earnings. First, he should reduce discretionary spending each month. This does not mean reduce to zero, but does mean making some conscious changes in where, how frequently, and how many dollars are going out the door for entertainment. Freeing up $400 to $500 a month would yield an incremental $5,000 to $6,000 in annual cash savings for an emergency fund or vehicle purchase.

Second, Jim should think creatively about his vehicle obligation. The high-end car and associated ~$500 lease payments each month are a noose to long-term savings. Selling the vehicle after a year of focused savings and buying a reliable used car would significantly improve his risk profile. What options are there to terminate a car lease? The expensive path is to return the car to dealership but there are fees associated with this so the change to a different vehicle has to present a very significant savings to make this a sensible options. Another option is to buy the car out from the leasing company. Here too, the buyout value can be expensive for a high end vehicle and stretch beyond the available capital Jim has. A more feasible option is to find someone to assume your lease, for which there are several online companies that help facilitate a legal transfer. Carefully evaluate the terms of the transfer to understand if you are still liable for the vehicle after the transfer in the event of the new lease payer defaults. Finally, the cleanest option is to sell the vehicle using the lease buyout price as a guide for what amount of money you owe to the leasing company. You may incur some loss here to complete the transaction but that cost may be worth it in the long term. An example: if the vehicle is a $45,000 luxury car and the buyout price of the lease is $34,000 but the used car private transaction resale value averages $30,000 from Kelly Blue Book's guidance, you may have to come up with the $4,000 difference in cash to accompany the $30,000 vehicle sales price in order to buyout from the lease company and complete the sale to the new owner fully. This is a complex transaction, but is a way to remove the monthly payment burden.

Third and finally, Jim should consider his luxury apartment rental at ~$1,500 a month plus utilities. While nice, riddled with amenities, and new construction, Jim is devoting a large portion of income to housing expense while building no equity. Although he has no maintenance costs, he is also quite literally throwing away the money. He should look at renting out the second bedroom to a responsible roommate to reduce his net monthly expenses. Or, he should consider relocating at the end of his lease to a lower cost rental – freeing up income for longer-term savings, like a down-payment on a starter home. Each of these changes would dial in a balanced risk profile that will help ensure long term financial sustainability and self-sufficiency.

Case Study 3:

Meet Craig and Sherri. College sweethearts, they have both focused on their corporate careers now for ten years. They are a couple of years from being ready to start a family and are focused on the work hard –

play hard lifestyle. Their combined incomes are $175,000 and they represent the epitome of the Dual Income, No Kids, or DINK class. Sherri just leased a BMW 5 series and John has had a leased sporty Cadillac. They settled in two years ago to their $350,000 mid-west dream home.

How does their budget work?

- Gross Monthly Income: $14,500
- Automatic Deductions for health insurance and taxes: $5,000
- Net Pay: $9,500
- Obligations for car and house: $3,200
- Other required expenses (e.g. groceries, utilities, property insurance, student loan debt etc.): $2,000
- Long-term goals (e.g. vacation, home repairs, car repairs, and retirement): $2,000
- Discretionary funds remaining: $2,300 – which lets them spend frequent weekends away and several nights a week eating out with friends at posh restaurants

What risks are John and Sherri implicitly taking on? Their finances and lifestyle choices assume that they will continue to drive a similar level of income for the foreseeable future. Although they have amassed $15,000 in emergency cash, this would realistically only last them three months given their required expenses, including the house and car payments.

Similar to the prior case studies, what if either lost a job with no severance and no or limited unemployment income? Their ability to quickly adjust required expenses is limited given it would necessitate downsizing to a smaller home or selling a leased vehicle.

What if they had a significant house expenditure, like a broken air conditioner or a need to replace old siding or a roof? They would be reliant on the same pool of emergency cash unless they had other less liquid invested savings. The point here is their current lifestyle illustrates they are dialed too high on discretionary spending and made some luxurious life decisions that have them over-obligated.

How could John and Sherri de-risk and set

themselves up to be ready to start a family on a firm financial footing, with a more limited downside risk from the impact of job loss? They could make a couple of key changes in the upcoming months. First, evaluating their discretionary spending habits and making a modest adjustment would generate enough savings in several months to purchase a used vehicle for cash.

Second, they should think hard about the need to have two leased luxury vehicles. Reducing to one, if not no leased vehicles, and instead purchasing cars they can pay cash for to remove the long-term obligation is a straightforward means to de-risk their finances.

Third, and particularly if they stretched to buy their dream home with a minimal down payment and 30 year mortgage, they should carefully consider their housing. The dream home inherently has larger long-term upkeep expenses as it ages on a square footage basis alone. Should a job loss occur, it is not merely the mortgage John and Sherri have to cover but also the utilities and upkeep. Taking $1,000 a month for the leased vehicles out of their obligations (assuming they made a change to used vehicles purchased with cash), their emergency savings would still only cover up to 4 months of obligated expenses.

Finally, they should spend effort to build their emergency reserve funds. To be clear, these are not investments for long-term retirement. The reserve fund ought to be highly liquid with low risk of loss. Each of these changes is readily possible with a few tweaks of the dial to their lifestyle.

Case Study 4:

Meet Billy Jean and Bob. In their mid-30's, they have one child with another on the way and are living on $40,000 of gross income. They are hard-working American's who are providing for their children and try to make their finances line up every single month. They have a single used car they paid for in cash and own outright. They live in a smaller 1000 square foot house they bought three years ago and watch each dollar. Billy Jean stays at home to care for their child and prepare for the newborn's impending arrival.

How does their budget work?

- Gross Monthly Income from Bob's job: $3,300
- Automatic Deductions for health insurance and taxes: $1,200
- Net Pay: $2,100
- Mortgage: $600
- Other required expenses (e.g. groceries, utilities, property insurance, children, etc.): $800
- Long-term goals (e.g. vacation, home repairs, car repairs, and retirement): $550
- Discretionary funds remaining: $150 – that is $37 a week left for Billy Jean and Bob to have a simple date night if they are fortunate enough to have their family watch their child.

These two have diligently saved $6,600 a year for a number of years as they worked towards their long term goals. They are frugal with their income, spending smartly and only when they can. Over the years, they have built an emergency cash savings fund of $12,000, separate from retirement accounts. Given their required expenses of $1,500 per month, they have an 8 month cushion which leaves them adequately prepared for an unexpected job loss.

What risks do they face? Given their growing family, Billy Jean and Bob need to ensure they have the right insurance policies in place should one of them unexpectedly be unable to work, or worse. The value of the insurance policy must be large enough to cover their debt obligation on the house and provide sufficient enough future income to support the rest of the family at least until the kids are independent. This will cost them some money each month to put in place, but it is well worth the peace of mind. Otherwise, they have sufficiently considered their finances and ensured they haven't over adjusted their discretionary spend dial, or under adjusted their savings dial.

These case study examples illustrate the delicate balance between income, obligated expenses, discretionary expenses, and savings and how the budget, cash flow, and net worth tools empowers each of us to dial in a profile that enables financial independence and self-sufficiency. While tempting to grow our required expenses to enjoy luxurious trappings of life, wouldn't you have a greater sense of pride and self-worth knowing that should something unexpected happen, you had done enough to manage through the challenge on your own? Read on to the next chapter as we close on some of the new tenants of financial responsibility for our modern world.

CHAPTER 7

THE NEW TENANTS OF FINANCIAL RESPONSIBILITY

The world is a dramatically changed place in the past ten years. Technology has made information instantly accessible and modified the way we work and socialize. The financial world is increasingly volatile with record low interest rates, bail outs, bail ins, quantitative easing, and other inventive approaches to supposedly forcing economic growth. Government services have record high number of payees as the disability, food stamp, Social Security, Medicare, and Medicaid rolls have expanded. The Wall Street Journal, leveraging data from the US Census Bureau, shows in the chart below how this government program dependence has changed over just the last 30 years.

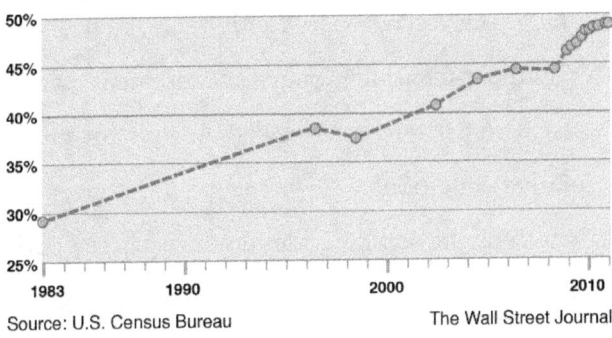

Stretching the Net

Percentage of U.S. population living in a household receiving some government benefit

Source: U.S. Census Bureau   The Wall Street Journal

In this context, increasingly important is understanding the new key tenants of financial responsibility so you are fully independent. To think that the government will always be a safety net not just to the Baby Boom generation, but also to the Millenials and Gen Y / Xers is unrealistic. As part of the younger generations, we have a responsibility to reverse the ever blossoming trend of government expenditure and we can readily do so by ensuring our own financial independence, living fully within our own means.

The Tenants

- You must still pay yourself first by putting money aside for short and long term savings before filling your discretionary fund.
- You must set aside money for retirement, and not just 5 to 10% to realistically account for current market conditions.
- You must be setting aside money each pay period for once per year expenses, like property taxes.
- You must be setting aside money for unexpected expenses like vehicle repairs or required home maintenance.
- You must be setting aside money for future vehicle expenditures. You need to be buying your car outright so you are purchasing what you can afford on prior income, not betting on future income. One exception is 0% financing deals that can occasionally be found. However, you should still have the full amount of cash in the bank or a guaranteed future income stream to sign-up for

these multi-year payment obligations.
- You must be thinking forward to other life goals. Are you expecting to get married, to move, to start a family? Are your savings plans adequately accounting for these future activities?
- Do you have outstanding debt besides a mortgage payment? If yes, you must develop a plan within your budget to pay it down and off as quickly as possible and at the sacrifice of your discretionary spending and in balance with building an emergency fund.
- Do you have a mortgage or are you looking to acquire one? Is your monthly payment greater than 20% of your take home pay? If yes, you must pay particular attention to building your emergency fund. If you have a loss of income, you must have a larger emergency cushion to maintain your mortgage payment obligation since it takes a large portion of your current income.
- Now I am not a survivalist, but do you have some money stowed away at home along with other emergency supplies to ensure you and your family is prepared for any unexpected disruptions caused

by natural events or other occurrences? If you cannot confidently say yes, you must include this preparation expense in your emergency fund obligation.

- On obtaining a traditional college education:
    - You need to work your way through to avoid as much debt as possible.
    - You need those scholarships to reduce your potential debt, so study hard. The payoff is your path to accelerated debt freedom.
    - You need to pick a degree and institution focused on getting you job-ready skills
    - Finally, if you are not ready to do the above, you should not be enrolling.

ABOUT THE AUTHOR

Mr. Webb is a seasoned wireless industry executive. He has led work efforts at Tier 1 North American Telecommunication corporations from strategy development to pre-consumer launch evaluation and certification testing across several key technologies.

He is also a knowledgeable personal finance resource with a keen focus on empowering others to learn the tools that enable long term financial success. From business travel across the United States to leisure travels around the world, he has observed enumerable approaches to personal finance that inform his unique point of view.

Mr. Webb resides in Overland Park, Kansas, with long-time partner, Jason, and their two dogs.

www.ingramcontent.com/pod-product-compliance
Lightning Source LLC
Chambersburg PA
CBHW071812170526
45167CB00003B/1274